Table of Contents

Robert G. Fritchie

Robert G. Fritchie

Introduction

This book continues where my previous book *Surviving Chaos: Healing With Divine Love* left off. In the year since *Surviving Chaos* was published, there have been significant changes throughout the world that reinforce the need for the solutions laid out in that book.

In *Apply Your Birthright* we are going to examine several important threats to our health stemming from the foods we eat, plus other sources. We will identify factors frustrating problem correction so that you will better appreciate how important Divine Love is to your health recovery.

You will learn advanced healing techniques that you can use to help yourself and be of service to mankind. Lastly, we will show you how we have applied our own teachings in several international group efforts to help correct worldwide health issues.

Sadly, we are in a time of great peril. We are being threatened by self-extinction from poor business decisions made over the last one hundred years. Some of those decisions failed to consider the potential for detrimental effects on human health. Now, people are suffering because of those decisions as evidenced by obesity, cancers, diabetes and other life threatening diseases that manifested.

The real tragedy is that what is happening right now has been withheld from the public. Fortunately, people are beginning to awaken to the perils and are starting to demand solutions.

In later chapters you will learn about a new paradigm coming into existence that can do a lot to help relieve the current situation.

Chapter 1

The Status
Of Human Health

Effect Of Foods

We are witnessing a marked deterioration in human health from the effects of foods that we consume. One of our worst health problems comes from the abundance of sugar in everything we eat.

Surprisingly, French citizens eat almost the same branded products that we eat in the U.S. with several key exceptions. French food does not contain the same quantities of raw white sugar and sugar substitutes as is found in our food and drink.

The human body can safely handle only a limited amount of raw sugar and sugar from corn syrups. When we exceed that safe amount consistently, our blood sugar content increases rapidly to levels that are unhealthy for us over the long term. When our bodies can no longer handle the continuing overload, sugars play havoc in our system by initiating health defects ranging from obesity to diabetes.

One way to protect your health is to become aware of what you are consuming. To get started, if a food does not meet the guidelines published in any good health book, *stop buying that food* and *complain* to the manufacturer. If only a few complaints are heard, there will be very little corrective action. However, if product sales suddenly drop, be assured that a company will modify its behavior and adjust its formulations.

You can utilize the healing principles taught in this and other World Service Institute books to correct a health issue, but you must accept responsibility for your own health. In the case of your food and body products, responsibility means that you read product labels, evaluate all content, and stop consuming things that are known to adversely affect health.

Consider the prevailing advice on fats. It has become well know that omega 6 fats are contained in many foods. Too much omega 6 fats are not good for you. Overload your system and soon your body will start to malfunction.

Instead, dieticians advise that we should consume more omega 3 oils obtainable from certain types of fish. Sounds good until you look at the source of the fish!

Toxic chemicals are continually being introduced into many inland fish farms via groundwater runoff. Most oceans now have unacceptable levels of heavy metals and chemicals that are toxic to the seafood we love to eat.

What to eat becomes increasingly complex with no assured solutions in the short term, except for healing ourselves and the environment. *We will explain how to achieve these healings in later chapters.*

Effect Of Chemicals

While dietary changes are recommended in every book on health and weight control, it would also be wise to increase your *awareness* about food source production and storage techniques. As you identify detrimental foods learn which support groups are opposing the questionable products. Join a group in demanding that those manufacturers produce safe products.

Otherwise, your only option is to buy organic products. Organics are certified to be 100% free of chemical fertilizers and contaminants, but add significant cost to your food bill. *Or you might take a low cost spiritual approach to purifying food that we will discuss later.*

In January 2010, newspapers reported

that some corn syrups are being contaminated by mercury introduced during the manufacturing process. Our average annual consumption of mercury can far exceed safety standards when we consider all the foods we eat containing corn syrup. We should not be ingesting mercury from any foods, but we are.

Look at your food labels and determine which products contain corn syrup. Next do your homework. The referenced news article stated that there were still four plants supplying food companies with mercury contaminated ingredients. Find out which food manufacturing plants are still using corn syrups made from a process involving mercury compounds.

Then determine which food companies use those contaminated syrups. Do your homework; identify branded products that you use that contain mercury contamination. Decide for yourself what is in your best interest.

It is known that mercury attacks DNA,

but determining the cumulative amount that will trigger a problem in a given body may vary from person to person. What is known is that mercury is entering the food chain through a variety of sources in alarming quantities. We are playing with food time bombs that can destroy us!

In February 2010, a news article appeared stating that several manufacturers are removing zinc from their dental adhesive formulations. Consumers are apparently using so much adhesive to hold in their false teeth that they are incurring massive exposure rates to the zinc. Lawyers filed lawsuits because they claimed that the zinc has caused neurological damage and blood problems in consumers, allegedly crippling some.

The irony is that under normal application the zinc content met government safety guidelines.

On March 2, 2010, news reports stated that many commercially sold fish oils contain the carcinogen PCB. PCB was dumped into waterways for many years and has made its way into the ecosystem along with many other toxins.

Are you getting the message here? *We are being poisoned by consumed toxins.*

Inhaled Toxins

The danger from polluted gases in major cities is great. How much "junk" air you breathe varies by the gases released into the atmosphere from all of the manufacturing plants, animals and vehicles. One thing is certain. None of the pollutants are good for you. When you can see or smell the pollution that you are breathing, it is time to take a sanity check on where you are living.

You can lobby for legislation, but you should know that your complaint will not be acted upon unless everyone involved agrees. As things stand right now, pollution control is simply too costly for a given company to implement a solution in every state where their products are made.

Disregard For Human Consequences

Harmful toxins are sometimes being introduced in the food growing cycle, the preparation cycle, and the storage cycle before food is sent to your favorite grocery store. You can learn about all these problems from many good books on the market.

Don't get me wrong. I am not suggesting that manufacturers are introducing any poisons to food on purpose. Rather, the problem is that additives are generally made to improve yield, shelf life, appeal, taste and so forth - without thoroughly knowing what the combination of chemicals have on human health.

As a society, we have fallen into very poor habits. We have a sense of entitlement that our condition is caused by someone else and that all we have to do is to take medicine to be well again. How will you feel when you learn that the illness you have comes from food toxicity that you could have avoided?

How Energy Works In The Body

All of the things we eat, touch, consume or breathe have various levels of contamination associated with them. We can be poisoned by many toxins every day without our knowledge. The effects upon our bodies can be catastrophic and may result in early death.

Think about this. We live what we think is a normal life. One day we feel poorly. A visit to a doctor reveals that we have "suddenly" developed a disease that over time may be fatal. Surgery, radiation or medicines might or might not, be a solution. How do you think that you will feel under those circumstances?

Sure - efforts to change the way we live are sometimes effective if an illness is caught early. All too often it is already too late. You should know that once your endocrine system is compromised, restoration is very doubtful. Why wait until you have a life-threatening illness before you change how you live?

Toxins interfere with our body chemistry. Toxins *produce energy and chemical disruptions* in our bodies. Once that happens, our blood, organs, glands, and nervous systems can go out of balance electrically, electromagnetically and biologically. These disruptions prevent our cells from operating normally and the cells mutate or die. Also, bacteria and viruses already existing in an inactive state in our body can suddenly activate. The result can be the manifestation of a variety of diseases. Sounds pretty bleak and it is!

The purpose of this chapter has been to make you aware of our mutual predicament. No one is out to get you, poison you, or kill you intentionally. However, we are all at risk through our collective ignorance - so everyone suffers.

A Spiritual Model

It is simply not possible to correct all of the aforementioned problems affecting mankind in a few years. We need to acknowledge our dilemma. We need solutions such that people can energetically do something right now to protect their health and maintain their life spans.

Our solution is to utilize a spiritual energy healing Process to affect change in both ourselves and our environment. The name of that Process is the Divine Love Group Healing Process (DLGHP).

Such broad changes may sound very ambitious. If we can agree that the DLGHP works and is a real solution, how do we use it in the face of all the opposition to change?

To better understand this spiritual model, we need to go back to 1980. We will look at what happened to me as my spiritual path transitioned from an engineer and businessman to that of a facilitator

Robert G. Fritchie

and researcher in energy healing. My transition story will help you to understand the reality and energetic power inherent in using the DLGHP.

Let me make the case for the DLGHP. Then decide for yourself if you want to continue as is, or be part of a solution for a better existence for yourself, your family and the rest of mankind.

Chapter 2

Back To The Beginning

The Creator

Most people believe in the existence of an unseen Architect of the universe that we call God, the Creator, or by some other name depending upon belief systems. That Creator is at the heart of all existence both on this planet and elsewhere in the universe.

Some people do not believe in a Creator and think that the Divine is best seen in nature. Yet these folks also recognize an unseen energy as part of what drives the world.

We will not quibble about the Who, the

Robert G. Fritchie

What, or the Where of the Creator. The Creator is a mystery throughout the universe.

Yet, there is something very important happening that we can all grasp without becoming embroiled in any form of religious controversy.

There is a phenomenal change occurring in human consciousness. People are now awakening to true spiritual realities that will replace the illusions with which they previously lived.

People who are on a spiritual path realize that there is other intelligence in the universe. For example, many people are able to communicate with unseen intelligence through enlightened beings, angels, guides, etc.

The public is generally in awe and simultaneously in fear of any spiritual contact whose origin is unknown. They fear that the contact may not be from their Creator.

Instead of investigating, determining and embracing the spiritual truth, some people hold on to their limited belief systems. They rely instead upon information that fortifies their existing beliefs.

Some of the public's concerns are valid. It is not logical to think that every intelligence is here to be our friend, but there is no need to be fearful. *We will teach you how to discriminate between spiritual and physical truth.*

The Universal Life Force

Most spiritual people know that there is an energy in the universe that is responsible for life itself. That energy force emits a three-second energy pulse that keeps all in existence. Some of you can tune into this pulse and experience it for yourself.

More important is the realization that without this pulse, most lifeforms would cease because the universal life force provides cell energy to our bodies.

When we are shut of from that life sustaining pulse, our cells stop functioning normally. When that happens, our cells lose memory and can begin to grow erratically, mutate into diseases or die.

In a well person, the universal life force automatically maintains our body energy level and keeps us in full energetic balance. All of this happens without a belief system or personal involvement. It is a mystery of life.

Many cultures recognized this life force and named it ki, chi, and prana to name a few. However, many of those cultures limited the use of the life force according to their beliefs or traditions. The full power of the universal life force was not experienced.

People that honor the Creator call this same energy Divine Love. The primary differences are: Divine Love is accepted as coming from the Creator in a neutral state.

It is an <u>unlimited</u> *healing energy* that can be utilized to create change. Divine Love is *activated by spiritual intention and acts* on our *Petition* (request).

From Raw Energy To Divine Love

The following historical narrative is true. It is provided so that you can grasp an important concept - the true meaning and application of Divine Love.

When I first became interested in helping people, I had absolutely no idea what I was getting into. Many of my colleagues thought I was foolish to risk my hard-earned professional reputation by chasing after an elusive concept called *energy healing*.

Starting in 1979, I had the good fortune of developing a friendship with the IBM scientist Marcel Vogel. When we met, we were both at a crossroads. We had accomplished many goals in our respective lives, but wanted to help people more directly. A bond of friendship developed between us and I was invited to participate in a development project that would continue over many years.

Dr. Vogel told me that I needed to study energy before I participated in the development program. This struck me as odd.

My training was in chemical engineering. The closest I had come to a formal study of unseen energy was in engineering thermodynamics.

Vogel gave me a reading list of fifty rare books from all over the world. He told me to study all of them. Fortunately our city library system had lending arrangements with universities and I was able to source the books. These books included many foreign and very old texts about human energy fields. I quickly realized that my knowledge of human energy was woefully lacking in substance.

In addition, Vogel arranged interviews for me with scientists, medical doctors, sensitives and people who were able to deduce the condition of the human body just by looking at an individual. (Today anyone exhibiting this gift is called a medical intuitive.)

At first I thought many of their energy concepts were pure speculation. I came to respect all of these people because they were all loving, well intentioned and accurate! Believe me, it is a total culture shock to meet someone - who in a span of sixty seconds can tell you about your health issues with unerring accuracy!

I learned that there were unseen energy fields responsible for operation of the human body. We are composed of many energy layers, much like the layers of the common onion. These layers are capable of capturing and holding energy coming into the body - be that energy good or bad for a human being.

I learned that in the 1960's, European medical researchers were measuring and identifying electrical charges on the outside surface of human organs. It was generally believed that all these surface charges kept an organ in correct electrical balance and healthy. When a positive charge is pulled off the surface of an organ, it leaves the organ with a weak spot, subject to intrusion by anything else in the body. Today, the public hears about this same concept as "free radical damage" in the body.

From Europe, I was introduced to variable frequency machines that promoted rapid healing. These devices were able to measure disease frequencies.

When a disease frequency is applied to a person with a 180 degree phase shift or opposite polarity the disease in question is electrically neutralized, becomes inactive and is undetectable.

There are two problems with frequency devices of this kind. One problem is that the frequency must be both accurate and precise or an unwanted frequency can be introduced into the body with the potential for adverse effects. I personally knew several people that ignored this truth and paid for it with their lives.

The second problem is that the root cause of a disease is not eliminated energetically. If a health problem stems from a frequency originating in soul or mind, a frequency machine does not clear the root cause. This means that a flare-up can occur days, weeks, months, or years later.

Healers that I met were able to correct illness in people by a variety of methods. Healers used feathers, crystals, sound, herbs, lights, colors, their hands, or projected energy into a person in need. The techniques worked well on the people in their respective cultures. The common denominator in most of these techniques is the frequency at which the technique operates to correct a particular illness.

In 1980 it was obvious to me that the intention of a healer influenced the healing. My question was what was behind energy healing and how did "healing" really work. In fact, half-way through my nine months of study, I had more questions than answers!

Neutral Energy

One healing device interested me in particular because it was used in so many cultures - the natural quartz crystal. I started to carry a small clear quartz crystal with me, even though I did not know how to use it.

In my sixth month of interviews, Vogel asked me to go to Dallas and meet a well known psychic named Kay. Upon arriving at her house, I talked to her for a few minutes about Vogel's crystal development project and showed her my small pocket crystal.

Kay told me that she wanted me to meet a neighbor who was a Registered Nurse. The nurse had completely lost her hearing in one ear. When the nurse walked

in, Kay surprised me by saying "Take out your crystal and correct her hearing."
Without hesitation, I pulled out the crystal and placed it against the nurse's ear. I felt a vibration in the crystal that built in intensity and suddenly stopped.

The nurse looked at me wide-eyed so I asked her what was wrong. She burst into tears and said that she could hear clearly!

There were two very shocked people in Kay's living room that day, the nurse and me. I was stunned by two things:

My intuitive response. Neither woman had told me which ear was deaf - I just knew.

The rapidity of the healing.

When I returned to Marcel's home in San Jose and told him what had recently happened, he simply smiled, hugged me and reached into his own pocket. He withdrew a four-sided, hand-cut, quartz crystal with pyramidal ends, handed it to me and said to study its use. His teaching style was certainly unique!

On my way home that Sunday, I had to change planes in Chicago. A woman who walked across my path suddenly fainted and fell down before I could catch her.

Without hesitation, I pulled my healing crystal from my pocket, held it against her thymus and did deep breathing. Her eyes popped open and she said that she could feel energy coursing through her body.

After helping her to her feet, she told me that she was a physician. She asked what it was that I had done to her. I explained to her that I was just getting started on a development project on energy healing and had simply charged up her body energetically. She invited me to come to her clinic to work with her on difficult cases. I agreed.

A few weeks later a business trip was to

take me near her city so I called her. We agreed to see patients after I finished my engineering workday.

That evening I was introduced to about a dozen people, all of whom had serious health issues. Working strictly on intuition, I worked with the patients individually and all of them received instant relief from their illness. I realized immediately that I was receiving profound spiritual guidance.

A few weeks later I was back in San Jose comparing notes with Marcel. I received another surprise. It turned out that we were doing almost the same thing with our crystals. We continued to perfect technique and started to share our experiences by teaching health professionals what we had learned.

Vogel was a superb teacher. He would make a pointed statement then leave it up to me to observe, understand and apply what he meant. For example, early in my intense education he made two very

Robert G. Fritchie

startling statements:

Humans can transmit energy through space.
Energy follows thought.

To validate his statements, he took me into his lab at IBM where he had set up an experiment. Ten feet from his equipment he pointed a crystal at a photomultiplier tube and pulsed his breath. Immediately we saw a light flash appear on the monitor. I knew his comment-*humans can transmit energy through space* was real!

Next he showed me the results of an experiment that he was preparing to show to a group of medical doctors. Dr. Vogel wanted to repeat an experiment conducted by Cleve Baxter wherein Baxter connected a plant to a lie detector. As Baxter projected thoughts to the plant, the lie detector stylus oscillated rapidly.

Vogel spent months experimenting with a philodendron plant using a modified

EKG machine. Vogel was able to repeat Baxter's experiment and attain identical results. That would have been a ho-hum event except that Marcel Vogel repeated the experiment again while he was on a trip to India 5,000 miles away! The plant and the equipment were in his home!

A physician friend turned on the equipment at a specified time and Vogel *focused* on the philodendron with the intention of tearing a leaf. Immediately the recorder registered the event and the needle went off scale.

This experiment was repeated at different time intervals with identical results, thus proving Vogel's profound statement that *energy follows thought*. In today's terms the expression is - *we can influence things with our intention.*

Dr. Vogel was an expert in crystallography and microscopy. He developed his hand-cut quartz crystals based upon the geometry of the Kabbalah Tree of

Robert G. Fritchie

Life. His devices were four-sided and about five inches long. Each end was cut to a pyramidal point that was between 57 and 60 degrees.

These devices were energy amplifiers. They took on and amplified the vibration (frequency) of the user (facilitator). This enabled crystal users to transmit a high energy charge through a short distance to help facilitate an energy release in a client.

The Energy Of Personal Love

We learned that we could charge the crystal devices with an even higher energy if our intention included "love." For a year I used the energy of *personal love* in the development program.

The healings were successful and most of the people recovered from all kinds of debilitating diseases. However, I learned that when I used my own energy, I generally became very tired after only six successive healing sessions.

I knew that when fatigue occurred in me it was because my body energy level had dropped too low. I could recharge myself using breathing techniques, but still felt tired if I continued to facilitate healings throughout the week.

Vogel arranged for me to visit Dr. Norman Shealy at his pain clinic. Norm graciously gave me access to about twelve of his patients. My expectation was that the patients would be freed from their pain.

The results were abysmal. Not one person was helped! And I was exhausted.

It took me quite awhile to understand why no one was helped. At the time I knew that the patients wanted help, but none of them were processing energy in their bodies.

The results were clear. The question was what was going on and why. Two years were to pass before I had the complete answer.

Robert G. Fritchie

The first reason for the lack of success with Dr. Shealy's patients became evident a few weeks later on a field trip with John J. Adams, M.D. Dr. Adams accompanied me on a trip to Pennsylvania and Ohio to meet several of the physicians with whom I worked.

An odd thing had been happening with female patients. As they released discordant energy with the healing crystal, they experienced electrostatic shocks on their slacks or pantyhose. If they patted the area with their hand, the charge dissipated rapidly and they became well. The frequent electrical shocks, while not especially painful, were an annoyance. I was the only one of six people testing these early devices that experienced this effect.

Dr. Adams observed my technique and suggested that I might be using a limited definition of love in my work. Acting on that suggestion, we worked together to release me from my "limited beliefs concerning the energy of love."

The electrostatic effect did not reoccur in any client. My lesson was that *I had to be able to transmit energetic personal love without limiting that energy.*

Over the months ahead, I took on more clients with supposedly untreatable diseases and had excellent results with most of them. One day I was challenged by a frustrated mother.

She had brought her vomiting child to the physician with whom I was working that day. The mother didn't want me helping her child with a device, so I put the healing crystal aside and had the child climb up on my lap.

I realized that the child blamed himself for a fight that had taken place between his parents. I asked the child to take in God's love and he immediately responded. He stopped vomiting. Color returned to his face. He jumped down off my lap and scampered merrily out of the room! There were multiple teachings for me that day.

My own energy system had cleared to the point that I was able to transfer a high charge to an individual without using the healing crystal.

My sense of knowing the source of an individual's health issue had suddenly manifested. From that day on I had a sense of what was wrong with a client regardless of what they said, or did not say to me.

More importantly, it was evident to me that when the Creator's love was involved things happened rapidly.

The Energy Of Divine Love

Over the following months, I tested all of these teachings and realized that they were all true and applicable to the healing process. When I charged my healing crystal with Divine Love (the Creator's love), the amplified energy that was developed facilitated healings in people.

If I used Divine Love without the crystal,

the results were the same. My body had attained the amplified energy level of the crystal!

In 1982 a number of clients appeared that again were not processing energy. This time, I was able to intuit that they all had issues about loving the Creator, themselves and other people. If those limited beliefs were cleared first, clients were then able to successfully release the root causes of their illness - and they became well. *If the limited beliefs were not released first, healing efforts produced very limited results.* I called these limited beliefs *Life Lessons* and discuss nine of them in detail in Chapter 5.

I also observed that Divine Love literally dissolved any energy disturbance, provided that a client was willing to accept Divine Love! The answer to the lack of success with Dr. Shealy's patients was finally resolved. While I did not see any of Doctor Shealy's patients again, I did have ample opportunity to work with similarly afflicted people over the years.

Robert G. Fritchie

All were helped.

In 1983 I left my consulting engineering practice and moved with my wife to San Jose. We helped Marcel Vogel build a research facility in San Jose, CA, from which Marcel continued to study subtle energies for many years.

From the lab experience, I learned more about how to interact with human energy fields to more effectively release energy blockages that had accumulated in people. When blockages were correctly removed, a client's cells reset and were able to regain health.

Conversion From Crystal Healing To Spiritual Healing

Over the ensuing years, I continued lecturing in workshops across the U.S. and Eastern Canada as did Dr. Vogel and the other practitioners of crystal healing.

The next lessons came from the crystal devices themselves. It was getting very difficult to buy pure quartz crystals in the size and quality levels needed for the hand-cut healing crystals Vogel wanted to produce. Personal computers were in full development. Computer chip manufacturers everywhere rushed to secure a market source of raw quartz. Raw material costs rose rapidly and the price of a finished healing crystal became too expensive for many buyers.

Several things started to bother me. I observed that many crystal facilitators were becoming more interested in their reputation as a "healer" than in serving people in need of help. Also, some of the facilitators were emotionally attached to their crystal and saw it as some kind of a magical device. I viewed this attachment as a condition to be avoided because it did not properly credit the Creator for the results achieved. A healing crystal is a valid scientific tool.

As the years wore on, I switched emphasis to teaching the principles of Divine Love with non-crystal techniques to help people. This eliminated dependence on healing devices.

Most of my students lacked the energy to affect significant changes in themselves or others. Therefore, I started to teach Group healing concepts so that the entire Group energy could be applied to those recipients in search of a spiritual healing.

Development Of the Divine Love Group Healing Process

Over the next fifteen years, a repeatable healing method was exhaustively tested and perfected that I called the *Divine Love Group Healing Process* (DLGHP).

During my years of crystal healing, I noticed that people thought that a crystal facilitator had special powers. For instance, folks applied many labels to me like shaman, healer, or guru. I resisted the labels as they were blatantly incorrect, but I was not able to change their labeling practice.

One of my objectives in developing the DLGHP was to dispel the myth that any facilitator was all powerful. In this I was successful because once a Group learned the DLGHP fundamentals, they realized several key concepts:

We are all facilitators and not healers because *it is Divine Love that does all the healing, not us.*

We are not limited in our abilities to help others. What we lack in energy individually, we can compensate for by increasing the Group size because *Group energy output increases exponentially with more people.*

Profound things will usually happen in a Group where those seeking help accept the DLGHP as a s*piritual* process rather than a mental process.

During the development of the Process, I drew on all the information I had been exposed to in my training with Marcel, plus my many years as a researcher in

Robert G. Fritchie

energy healing development.

One of the most interesting aspects of my study was the concept of Soul. The ancient books all talked about Soul. As I studied and further tested Soul energy, I learned several important things:

When we are born we enter life with a Soul energy field that can be sensed and measured.

The *Soul* can carry with it vibrations from previous lives that limits the attainment of one's full potential in this life. This effect continues until the limiting vibrations are released from the Soul.

There is a higher energy form called our *Spirit*. It is attached to us like a high-security telephone link to the Creator. When Spirit is used in conjunction with Divine Love, a person is able to correct life-limiting vibrations coming from their own Soul, if they love the Creator.

Many mind/body teachers are satisfied operating in a mode without acknowledging Soul or Spirit. This is unfortunate because it limits their effectiveness.

In my research, several additional teachings emerged:

Mind energy can drain charge from a facilitator's body and mind energy is less effective in healing work.

Soul has a higher vibration level than mind. Thus Soul affords a higher energy with which to correct mind and the body.

Soul does not introduce fatigue in the facilitator and results are better with Soul energy rather than mind energy.

Your Spirit has a much higher vibration compared to Soul or mind. Thus, Spirit is the most effective energy form to use to facilitate the Petition in the healing of your Soul, mind and body.

Robert G. Fritchie

In Group work, a small group of Spirit-based people can produce a healing effect at an energy level that is many times more powerful than a same sized group comprised of Soul-based people.

When folks accept the reality of their own Spirit, they become spirit-based and become capable of transferring energy at much higher levels. (That is why we teach people to use Spirit in all that they do.)

Chapter 3

Current Thinking

Abbreviated History

There is a wide assortment of beliefs in the world that run the gamut from established religions to New Age thinking. In Judaic, Christian and Muslim beliefs, people worship the same deity according to the teachings of their key prophets and sacred texts. Other religions teach the importance of honoring nature, ancestors and master teachers. All of these traditions and religions span thousands of years. Yet many people find current religions unsuited to their modern lifestyles and beliefs.

Robert G. Fritchie

Thus, in the current culture of modernism, there has been a migration away from several organized religions. Some people even choose to go through their lives without a belief in a higher power in the universe.

Industrialized nations seem to be migrating towards less-formal belief systems that offer more spirituality. The fundamental principles of many of these spiritual teachings are to practice "spiritual love, compassion and forgiveness." Then as folks advance along a path towards higher spirituality, they hope to achieve peace and bliss here on earth.
Everyday life becomes less stressful and one is able to rise above one's current situation.

While these teachings have worldwide appeal, many people translate the teachings as *something to aspire to that lies outside or beyond themselves.*

There is another way of looking at man's current existence on this planet:

Apply Your Birthright

We are all Spiritual Beings that happen to have a physical body.

We are not just physical life forms seeking a spiritual identity. We already have a spiritual identity!

There is a spiritual birthright available to all of us because we are all sons and daughters of that Divine source we call the Creator. Therefore, if we choose to follow a spiritual path and see ourselves as a reflection of the Divine, we begin to realize that *we are not limited by our current physical existence.*

Rather, *we can learn to adjust our bodies and our environments to bring us into alignment with the Divine.* Alignment as used here is coincident with a return to health. We can attain alignment through the acceptance and right use of the Creator's life force. We call that life force Divine Love. We are able to achieve our alignment because Divine Love is the most powerful healing energy in the universe.

53

Robert G. Fritchie

Again, Divine Love is an *unlimited energy source* existing in a neutral state. It can be activated with intention by those people that operate in conjunction with the Creator.

There are several differences in what we are teaching compared to what religions and other spiritual teachers may offer.

Our teachings are that:

We are all able to *experience* Divine Love as a real life changing energy.

We can *all engage directly in an energetic healing Process* to change self and the environment.

We accept full *responsibility* for ourselves and the world.

We *love, honor and respect the Creator* to the best of our ability.

We see *Divine Love as an all encompassing energy* that includes all the prophets, Masters and angels without exception.

We can l*earn to focus Divine Love onto or into a physical target, be it a* person, place, or thing and *help facilitate a change* in that target.

As we learn to release that which has limited our *awareness*, our bodies become *spiritually aligned* with the Creator. Then we are able to correct things that have made us unwell.

Misinterpretations

Thousands of years ago, ancient civilizations of the Middle East were defined in the Bible as the "known world." Even before Biblical times, there is evidence that civilizations existed in other parts of the world as well.

Interestingly, these earlier civilizations went through a growth phase and were later presumably destroyed by cataclysmic events that ranged from asteroids striking earth, tectonic plate adjustments, volcanic eruptions and the sinking of entire continents. Scientists claim the earth is now in its fifth rotation of civilization.

In the infancy of the world religions, the Master Teachers understood the Divine. They knew precisely how to apply universal life forces to make adjustments in nature and human beings.

The Masters efforts were widely seen as supernatural because the populace did not understand what they were observing. Since the public could not do the same thing, they proclaimed that all healing observations had to be miracles. *(The same thinking prevails today, that is, until people learn that they can do the same things. Then it becomes an "aha" moment and people start to embrace spiritual healing.)*

Ancient civilizations developed a variety of healing methods that were unique to their locale. For example:

Thousands of years ago a healing art developed in China that was based upon movement of energy through the human body. Westerners scoffed as Chinese doctors produced amazing results. Today the whole world benefits from acupuncture and Chinese medicine.

An ancient healing method was preserved for centuries by shamans and is now reemerging as Ho'Oponopono, the Hawaiian healing system. The key principles include: the practitioner of the art being personally *sorry*, asking *forgiveness* for whatever is going on *in the practitioner* that is *responsible* for whatever condition is *manifesting* in a client, plus the statement- *I love you.*

India developed a system of healing called Ayurveda that is based upon giving people the food groups, herbs and exercises needed to balance their system. Today Ayurveda is spreading as this system of healing is shared in many Asian countries.

Each of the indigenous tribes of the world have spiritual leaders who are able to identify and utilize things in nature to help their people to recover from illness. Indian medicine men throughout the Americas have techniques and remedies that work.

As ancient civilizations matured or died off, healing methods were passed on. However, the willingness to share knowledge became very guarded as practitioners sought personal power or attempted to hold on to their elevated social status. What was once widely known became a mystery known only to a few.

In some countries sophisticated healers became targets of oppression because the rulers and religious leaders of their countries were afraid of losing control over the populace. It is obvious that fear and old limited belief systems have not helped humanity.

The early history of the U.S. was marked by religious persecution of colonists during the Salem witchcraft trials. Dozens of people were condemned to death on the whims of neighbors making false claims.

Religious intolerance continues in many parts of the world today, thereby promoting an atmosphere of suspicion and distrust.

Dealing With Reality

Today the general public is more open to understanding energy healing since the topic is broadly discussed. People are all seeking alternatives that give them more personal control over their wellness.

Science is also awakening to new energy realities that were previously thought to be impossible. Examples of this are seen in quantum physics where current discoveries are being made that can not be explained in our three dimensional view of life. It is now clear that particles can appear and disappear and that "twin" particles can suddenly appear that were not part of an experiment. Some scientists have even suggested that maybe we live in a parallel universe!

Science uses a rigorous method of investigation. First a hypothesis is formed. Then experiments are run to prove the hypothesis. However experiments can be seriously flawed. It has been shown that an experimenter can affect results by contaminating the experiment with the energy of his/her own thought. Then what we get are results that are not the truth.

Interestingly, spiritual energy healing using the DLGHP is NOT affected by a negative intention from someone that would attempt to interfere with a Divine Love healing.

Sadly, scientific and medical researchers are put under a lot of pressures that include: need for recognition, more project funding, "a rush to find the cure", higher profits and so forth. This has led to non-acceptance of new energy technologies because those technologies threaten the status quo.

Consider what might happen if we all wake up tomorrow morning and some "phenomenal discovery" has been announced that proclaims:

Here is the answer to all disease! Here is the answer to world health problems!

Massive opposition would be instantly expressed because:

Medical or research specialists might no longer be needed in their accredited field of study.

Much of the medical diagnostic and measuring equipment might become unneeded.

Instead of medical doctor shortages around the world, there might be sufficient physicians to supply medical

61

assistance to people worldwide.

Pharmaceutical companies could reduce research on new drugs thereby maximizing profits.

Psychiatry might switch to a different teaching and treatment platform.

Cancer research might possibly become obsolete.

Surgeries might greatly diminish and the need for specialists might shift to other fields.

Open heart surgeries and bypass surgeries might become less frequent.

Hospitals could process more people with less sophisticated equipment.

Other talented resources might become more evenly distributed around the world.

Some charities might be unneeded.

Insurance companies might have less customers and decreased claims with potentially decreased revenue.

For the reasons stated above, nobody can implement *any kind* of a worldwide solution to the revolutionary new "phenomenal discovery" because somebody will feel threatened and object.

Are you beginning to see the need for a change yet? Perhaps we need to explore three questions to drive home the point.

Pop Quiz

Question One: *While you and I might enjoy less health costs, how long do you think rapid healing techniques would be tolerated by those individuals whose primary focus is to generate a profit?*

Not very long right? So what we are facing is a paradigm shift in how spiritual healing, medicine and alternative healing methods can all peacefully coexist to help people. This would need to be implemented without exposing people to charlatans, quacks or methods that lead to early deaths through errors and unworkable treatments.

Question Two: *How do we get to this new level of holistic healing service short of restarting civilization after a catastrophe?*

The answer to this question is the entire point of this book. Why should society even consider a new paradigm?

The paradigm is necessary because we are no longer able to avert deterioration in the world, both in terms of increasing health failures and the destruction of the earth through pollution. We will examine some of these problems and show you how to effect a peaceful solution for the betterment of all people.

Question Three: *What health evidence exists that shows that we really are spiraling out of control?*

In his well written book, *Anti Cancer, A New Way of Life,* researcher David Servan Schreiber, M.D., PhD, identifies what the latest cancer research has uncovered. He shows that the Western diet has contributed to a much higher incidence of cancer in the U.S. than is found in other countries.

For example, recently published studies have shown that cancers are seven to sixty times more prevalent here in the U.S. than in most Asian countries. Some European countries increased cancers by 60% in just the last twenty years!

He went on to reveal that those who ate low sugar content meals, as is found in Asian diets, tend to have five to ten times fewer cancers than those folks eating excessively sugared and refined foods. Too much refined sugar in the diet is known to raise insulin levels.

In 2009 a Women's Health Initiative study of postmenopausal women confirmed a link between increased insulin levels coming from high sugar diets and white flour. The study showed an increased risk of breast cancer that was twice the norm.

One of the continuing problems is that many cancers exist that do not respond to an established regimen of medications. The same phenomenon is seen in AIDS virus mutations. Also bacterial infections like MRSA (a treatment resistant staph infection) are also highly resistant to treatment.

We are seeing an increase in diseases; some do not have medical solutions.

For example, during 2008 about 2.7 million people became infected with the human immunodeficiency virus (HIV) that cause AIDS. In the same year, 2 million people died from AIDS.

Treatment when available, slows but does not eliminate the virus. (Source: ALERT 2010.) The health industry has not promoted a simple way to correct these diseases, but several exist.

The current medical model is treatment of symptoms based upon lab tests or the doctor's diagnosis. However *the energetic root cause of an illness is not treated and removed. This is because medical science has neither understood nor generally accepted that a human being is composed of energy fields that when energetically corrected, enables a body to heal itself naturally.*

This is where spiritual healing can help facilitate a solution. *We do not have to know what the root cause is or where it is located.* What we do is use *our* Spirit to identify where the energy associated with the disease source is located --and release that source energetically with Divine Love. Then as needed, treatments to restore the body through balanced nutrition, medicine or other modalities become more effective.

In the world of chemistry, polychlorinated biphenyls (PCB), dioxins and polybiphenols are all cancer producers. We take in these toxins mostly through the foods we eat. The foods can get contaminated during production on toxin-laced lands or from contaminated water.

These same toxins are now very severe in major oceans. Fish and crustaceans are dying and are becoming so contaminated that we can not use them for food. Admittedly, there are many other pollution sources killing ocean life, but you get the general idea.

The prescribed medical treatment for eliminating most toxins is very limited because there are few to no treatments that actually get toxins out of the body. At best, some toxins are tied up in our body fat awaiting their chance to interfere with our cells. *Conversely, many clients have been able to safely detoxify using the DLGHP.*

Chapter 4

Unification Of Humanity

Placing Value On Life

Throughout the ages mankind has abused power. This has been done through manipulation, ideologies, and disregard for human life starting thousands of years ago - even before the Great Pyramid was constructed. As man evolved, some people chose the path of honoring life. Others chose to disregard the lives of their fellow man to satisfy their personal goals. Both practices are still with us in full force.

However, we are seeing a major leveling taking place. Nations are experiencing chaos that threatens their very survival. Sure, any dissident can set off a bomb that kills thousands of people, but that is not the point.

The point is this. People are being subjected to shortages of food and potable water. We are also experiencing environmental poisoning that is affecting our DNA our lives and the lives of our children. These problems are worldwide.

I have heard people argue that the world is overpopulated anyway, so a forced reduction in population leaves more for the survivors. Those thinkers are missing a key point that is:

> If they are one of the survivors, what makes them think that they will be able to live in a contaminated world?

Like it or not, the paradigm shift to a more spiritual life has already begun. Those that are truly spiritual know this to be true.

Spiritual people may know something else that you may not. *The vibration of Divine Love is increasing in the universe.*

Part of the transition to a new paradigm requires that you function as a loving person. People who honor the Creator will be able to endure whatever comes their way.

Fail to achieve that condition and you may find that it becomes very difficult for you. Simple functions will become nearly impossible because you will not be in energetic balance. People are already reporting lack of clarity, great difficulty thinking and overall sluggish feelings.

The evidence is before you right now. Look at the incidence of people shooting school children, church congregations, employers and spouses. Look at the increasing numbers of priests and teachers abusing children. Do you believe this behavior is a coincidence?

Robert G. Fritchie

Placing Value On The Environment

As we pollute we only hurt ourselves and future generations, so we obviously need to stop polluting. An additional question that needs to be answered is how to proceed *right now* to correct pollution that is already in our ecosystem. *The answer lies in water.*

Water is an unfolding mystery. Water is programmable and can store an energy charge. You can charge water with *love* or *Divine Love* using your intention.

Science teaches us that we humans are composed mostly of water. Divine Love can act on the water in our bodies and adjust that which is out of balance in us. The same thing can be done with ecosystem water throughout the world.

By using our Spirit, Divine Love, plus a proper intention, the properties of water (and food) can be altered anywhere.

Thus, until that day arrives when pollu-

tion solutions are a worldwide reality, we can act right now to preserve our future by utilizing the DLGHP to affect change. The detailed mechanisms to implement needed changes were presented in *Surviving Chaos* and will not be repeated here.

In the following chapters, we will show you *how* these changes can be made and what you need to do to participate in the healing Process effectively. First understand that you have a *birthright* given to you by the Creator. *Your birthright is the most important gift that you can experience and apply.* It is so important to you and to me that it is the title of this book.

Chapter 5

Solutions Made Possible

Spiritual Birthrights

There are many theories about why human beings exist and where we all came from. Some of the reasons offered are:

We are sent here to experience life and learn lessons before returning to the Creator.

We have all been deposited here by civilizations from other galaxies or planets.

We developed naturally from other life forms on earth such as apes and chimpanzees.

We all descend from Adam and Eve.

People argue over all of these concepts. Each person has a viewpoint based upon their sacred teachings. Fortunately there is a common denominator.

No matter how we got here and no matter what our purpose is in life, we are all products of the Divine, the Creator. *For that reason alone, every human being regardless of race, sex, age or national origin is entitled to say that they are a Son or Daughter of the Creator.*

Guess what folks? That makes us spiritual brothers and sisters as well! Therefore, every human being has the spiritual birthright to ask their spiritual father, the Creator, for help.

When you claim your birthright and begin to apply it, your world, your reality and your health will begin to change for the better. You however, must make the effort required!

Angels

As a child I exasperated my folks by questioning everything I was told. Most kids did the same thing to gain attention by asking "why" all the time. I did it to learn.

Like me, you were probably told that you had one or more Guardian angels or spiritual guides watching over you. In fact, many of my childhood friends told me they could actually see their angels when they were children. Most kids lost their "angel seeing" ability as they grew up because adults told the children that they were imagining the events!

To me this is a very interesting contra-diction. People claim to believe in angels, yet deny the angels when given an op-portunity to interact with them.

As a child I don't recall seeing an angel, but I do remember an unseen voice encouraging me. In the last thirty years, I have met many adults that see angels every day. It is not their imagination - it is the true reality!

I have never had a marijuana cigarette or recreational drugs. I tell you this to set the stage for my own angel encounters that I am revealing here publicly for the first time.

My first encounter was on a late Sunday afternoon in November of 1979. I was sitting alone in my dimly lit living room quietly reflecting upon my life.

I had already achieved most of the goals I had wanted. Yet I felt empty inside because I wanted to do something definitive to help more people.

My entire career had been spent satisfying company objectives that had little involvement with the general public. As I sat there, I made a mental commitment to do something to help people, but had absolutely no idea what to do or how to begin. So I asked my God to show me what he wanted me to do.

Immediately, I saw a three-dimensional holographic form of the Great Pyramid. It was about three feet in front of me, in color, and slowly rotating. A deep voice said: "Study energy." I was flabbergasted and didn't know what to think.

My wife returned from a shopping trip and asked me what was wrong. Apparently I was white as a ghost! It took me several hours before I could even tell her what had transpired. She listened to me, but said little.

A week later I spotted Marcel Vogel on a television program and made an instant connection to him. I called him at his home and the following weekend I was sitting in his living room discussing our mutual interests. I told him about my vision and he smiled sweetly and said we would work together. It was the beginning of a lifetime friendship.

In early 1980, I became aware of spiritual guidance in the form of angels who watched over me. The angels ran interference for me as I struggled to understand and apply the principles of Divine Love. These beings were always very loving to me. I could feel and even sense their presence even though I could not physically see them.

At first I was very skeptical of their input because whatever it was I was learning had to be in a form that could be taught to and implemented by other people. I also wanted to know that what I was doing was real and not just a figment of my imagination!

I was a chemical engineer that had received a rigorous training on how to approach problem solving and real world physical solutions. The very idea of an unseen world was foreign to me, so I moved forward slowly.

My reluctance to fully engage with dedication and enthusiasm was duly noted

Robert G. Fritchie

by the angels.

One late afternoon I was walking to my hotel after a long day with engineering clients. As I stood at a corner waiting for the traffic light to change, I heard a clear voice ask me if I wanted to see several demonstrations of the reality of the spiritual vs. physical world. Being a curious person, I readily agreed.

The voice said to me: "Take off your glasses and behold what a bee sees." As I recall, I saw the same image replicated in each eye in a four by four matrix, like stacking sixteen TV's - four high and four wide. These sixteen images of the same thing occurred in each eye. This certainly got my attention! I marveled at how clear the images were wherever I looked. This lasted about ten minutes and then the effect disappeared and my vision returned to normal. To think that an angel could alter my vision at will was certainly interesting.

As I entered my hotel room, the voice

said again: "Pull the shades and sit on the sofa." It was quite dark in the room with the shades drawn. Opposite the sofa about ten feet away was the closed entry door.

As my eyes grew accustomed to the dark, I saw a whirling light that appeared to be projected onto the door. The light came to a stop and I saw three very bright dots of white light positioned like the three points of a six inch equilateral triangle. Each dot was about the size of a dime.

Then the voice said: "Try to get up." I tried to move and couldn't budge. An invisible force held me firmly in place. It didn't hurt, but I couldn't even wiggle my fingers! Then the voice said again: "Be not afraid, I am the Alpha and the Omega." Then I was released and could move freely.

I was not fearful but I was most certainly in awe! Then I had the profound insight that what I was doing was God's work.

Robert G. Fritchie

A very comforting and serene feeling of total love enveloped me that I could feel both then - and today as this is written.

My appreciation for my angelic support deepened because I knew that all was as it should be. I dedicated myself with renewed interest to learn and apply all that I could. My only request was that whatever was to be learned had to be something that could be taught and implemented by others as well as me. I wanted cold hard facts that could be explained, not unprovable theories.

Angels led me to healing experiences to enrich my understanding of the Creator and help me to learn spiritual truths by trial and error. If I learned the lesson, I moved on to the next teaching. If not, additional experiences were given until I grasped the intended key spiritual point.

For example, I often asked myself how a particular energy healing mechanism actually worked. Within a few days, three or more clients would be presented to me that exhibited the *exact* problem I was interested in learning about! Every new symptom healing I was involved in was validated by triplicate cases.

Eventually I saw an emerging pattern of spiritual preconditions that I called *Life Lessons*. As people came to me, for help, we would work together to release them from the symptoms that they exhibited. Their symptoms always included one or more of the Life Lessons.

I concentrated on working with human Groups and did not teach angelic participation in healing, mostly because I wanted people to understand and take responsibility for their lives without becoming dependent on angels.

Midway through 2008, the energy of Divine Love started to increase in intensity. Many of my friends reported the same observation to me. At first I didn't concern myself about the energy increase because healing results were continuing normally.

However, by mid-2009 it was clear that the energy increase was affecting people dramatically. Clients began appearing with illnesses that had nearly immobilized them. Even when they tried to release a symptom, they often times could not. They were so overwhelmed by their trauma, panic, fear and depression that they could not even express themselves clearly. Energy would simply NOT flow in their bodies. In each case, the people had to release one or more spiritual Life Lessons before their original symptoms would correct.

The DLGHP Angel Petition

It was December of 2009. We were conducting public healing programs using Volunteer Groups. We were working on so many extremely difficult human and environmental problems that we chose to ask the Creator's angels for help implementing our Petitions. Our requests were granted and worked so well that we now use the following angel Petition in all of our activities.

With my Spirit and the angels help, I accept Divine Love and focus Divine love into my thymus. I surrender my will to the Creator's will. I acknowledge (Symptom Statement) and ask that the sources of these problems be released and corrected in my system with Divine Love according to the Creator's will.

The Nine Spiritual Life Lessons

The complex cases continued, so I prepared a tutorial for clearing out Spiritual Life Lessons. I asked recipients to apply each Life Lesson in a Petition.

Those people that invested their time experienced major changes in their lives. The majority of them became well.

Following is an abstract of that tutorial.

The DLGHP has been utilized successfully by thousands of people. You must however take full personal responsibility for attaining your own wellness.

Robert G. Fritchie

Sometimes when people use a Petition and do not get immediate results, they get discouraged and stop trying. Instead of quitting, look at illness as an indicator of something that you need to change in your life. Your illness is not punishment.

The Petition works well - provided that you do not have spiritual *blocks* that can inhibit the flow of Divine Love.

These *blocks* are in the form of *limited belief systems* that must be removed before you can get healing relief. Here are two conditions that may be frustrating your healing:

1. A *symptom* can have more than one *source (root cause)*. All sources must be removed to achieve a proper healing. Usually if you participate in a Group, the Group energy is sufficient to remove all of the SOURCES for a given symptom. When the symptom still remains, pay attention to the second condition below.

2. *Sources* may contain one or more

deeply-seated spiritual problems. These must be removed to attain wellness.

There are nine spiritual problems called Life Lessons (LL) that can inhibit your healing progress. They are spiritual because they can originate in Soul. An LL can also reside in the energy field called your mind.

Work on only <u>one</u> LL in any twenty-four hour period. Use the LL Petition shown below 5 times on each LL spaced out to fill a twelve hour period. Each time that you do an LL Petition, sit quietly for five minutes, then go about your business. (Do not start a new LL right before going to bed as the vitalizing energy may keep you awake.)

Wait twelve hours before starting a new LL. The reason for the twelve hour break is to give your body time to recuperate and rebuild. Do not rush this procedure as the effects can be profound and please do all the LL's in the order given. Do not skip around. The completion of

Robert G. Fritchie

all nine Life Lessons is one SET.

Do the nine Life Lessons by yourself. Be prepared to repeat the full SET of nine Lessons as needed because some of the effects can be deeply buried in your system and may not release completely in one pass.

Remember that your body progresses at a pace dictated by your Spirit and not by your active desires.

If you try to use your Petition and do not get relief from a symptom that you are exhibiting, *first seek help from a Group formed from family or friends.*

If you still do not get relief, then apply each of the following Life Lessons in an angel Petition, one-at-a-time until you clear all the Life Lesson conditions.

I prefer working in a support group with other people because the Group can validate your progress. Also, healing occurs more quickly. Know this about Group energy: All nine of your LL's can usually be done in one Group session. (Do each LL in its own Petition.)

You may have to repeat a Group set until you can confirm that all nine LL's are out of your system. Be sure to have your progress checked by your Group or do your own muscle test.

Here are the LL Statements to be used in separate DLGHP Angel Petitions.

All my:

1. Limited beliefs concerning a definition of the Creator.

2. Fears about the Creator, myself and other people.

3. Limited beliefs concerning Divine Love.

4. Limited beliefs about loving and being loved by the Creator.

Robert G. Fritchie

5. Limited beliefs concerning my own Spirit and Soul.

6. Limited beliefs concerning loving myself and loving and being loved by other people.

7. Feelings and beliefs about being abandoned by people or the Creator.

8. Fear of living a full life.

9. Limited trust of spiritual healing.

Life Lessons Discussion

Life Lesson 1: Limited beliefs concerning a definition of the Creator.

We have been exposed to a wide variety of ideas about the Supreme Being called God or the Creator. There are religious documents testifying to His existence, but very little information is given other than that He is all powerful and created everything.

In addition many people have been told that there is no Creator; still others once believed, but now do not.

To argue every case for and against a point of view is counterproductive. This LL statement is designed to surrender our opinions about the Creator and let Him infuse us with whatever information and definitions that He wants us to have.

Life Lesson 2: Fears about the Creator, myself and other people.

My personal belief is that the Creator is all loving for all His creations. You may have been brought up to believe that the Creator will punish you, take - kill - eat your children, or otherwise harm you if you don't love Him.

This LL is necessary because the thought that the Creator does not love you, or that you must love the Creator or be punished, induces a consummate FEAR buried deeply in your subconscious. As an adult, you may not even be aware of the fear. That fear will block you from releasing a symptom that you are trying to correct - until you first release your fear of the Creator.

Often times we are conditioned by family members or someone else who tells us that *we are not good enough* or *not worthy*. This crushes the average person and develops a subliminal fear about our self-worth and ability to function.

Similarly, if you have been severely traumatized by another person for whatever reason, there is a tendency to experience that same fear with other people with whom you interact: friends, fellow workers, or even family members.

Frequently people choose to lay blame on the Creator for the early death of a child, relative or friend. Sometimes a person incapacitated by an accident, or confined to a wheel chair, becomes very bitter and blames the Creator for their condition.

No matter what has happened to you, or someone you love, it is not the Creator's fault. If you are using the Creator as a scapegoat for your *anger* or *hate*, you limit yourself severely. Consider this - why would you expect the Creator to grant your Petition if you do not honor and love the Creator <u>unconditionally</u>? You cannot love and hate at the same time!

This is a major and very important life lesson. Please do not ignore this statement in defense of what you believe to be true. Allow your own Spirit to guide your spiritual development to give you freedom to honor and love the Creator.

Life Lesson 3: Limited beliefs concerning Divine Love.

No matter what you have read, are being told by anyone, or ferret out for yourself, your definition of Divine Love is still incomplete and may be inaccurate. This

Robert G. Fritchie

LL is to release the limited beliefs and understanding that you have about Divine Love so that spiritual and physical truth can be made manifest in you.

Life Lesson 4: Limited beliefs about loving and being loved by the Creator.

We tend to be confused about spiritual love because we can not see it. If you do not feel spiritual love there is no way that I can describe it to you. To say that you love the Creator is fine, but what does that mean to you? Do you love the Creator more than your family, friends and yourself? Or does *love* have a casual meaning to you - like a telephone call in which you say: "love you, goodbye?"

Whatever you think *loving the Creator* and *being loved by the Creator* really means, you are probably understanding only part of that two-way love. This LL is to clear out those limitations so that you can feel the Creator's love and give the Creator your love.

Life Lesson 5: Limited beliefs concerning my own Spirit and Soul.

To me Spirit is a connection to the Creator much like a private telephone connection. You can use your Spirit to talk to the Creator directly.

Soul is an energy form that you are born with that carries a vibrational history of lessons learned in this life and past lives. Unfortunately, the Soul can contain imprints that limit you in this life until they are removed. *You can remove Soul imprints with your Spirit and a Petition.*

This may all sound really far-fetched for you to believe. That is why this LL is so important. What you are asking for is to eliminate any confusion or misunderstanding so that the spiritual and physical truth can become known to you.

Robert G. Fritchie

Life Lesson 6: Limited beliefs concerning loving myself and loving and being loved by other people.

When we are having problems, it is easy to start thinking that nobody loves us. This limited belief is responsible for a lot of the self-deprecation, depression, lack of self-worth and bouts of self-loathing people feel today. Do not assume that if you are a narcissist that you have met this LL requirement because you must also be able to be loving to those around you as well.

We all need to acknowledge other people in our lives by giving our spiritual love to them and accepting their spiritual love for us. This is usually very difficult to do if we try to change ourself using mental techniques.

When we use the spiritual Petition, the change becomes achievable in a surprisingly short time. Then one can experience and understand the key differences between non-emotional spiritual love vs. emotional physical love.

Life Lesson 7: Feelings and beliefs about being abandoned by people or the Creator.

Many people feel they were abandoned in childhood or in adulthood. This belief can also develop in an unborn child.

As you go through life, it may be almost impossible to form lasting relationships with people because the fear of ever being abandoned drives your behavior. Instead there is a tendency to withdraw to a comfortable place where you cannot be hurt emotionally.

You may have been abandoned at some time in the past or present. The great news is that you do not have to live with that limitation.

The Creator has not abandoned you. You feel abandoned because you do not seek His help.

Life Lesson 8: Fear of living a full life.

To avoid facing up to the shortcomings in our lives, we compensate by holding on to fears that prevent us from completing our own healing. These fears are stored in Soul or Mind or both.

When people are willing to surrender themselves to the Creator for spiritual guidance, they can usually become well. However, some people choose to hold on to their illness because it is an obvious and defined event for which they compensate by being a victim to their circumstance. Surprisingly, a lot of people choose to be a victim rather than return to wellness. Generally people do this because they think it is a safer choice than facing the uncertainty of returning to society or family life where one must compete to survive.

Life Lesson 9: Limited trust about spiritual healing.

This Petition is about the uncertainty of embracing spiritual healing compared to trying an assortment of other conflicting modalities. For example, people with an eating disorder or other addiction may try a variety of therapies, but often get only limited improvement that does not last. They do not realize that their disorder can have a spiritual origin in need of healing. Drug and alcohol addictions can also have a spiritual origin.

Also certain food addictions are seen as comforting behavior during stressful or fearful events. Besides, who doesn't get enjoyment eating really yummy things like cakes, chocolate, pies and candies?

The danger is life-threatening. By eating candy, raw sugars and chocolate excessively, you upset your blood system. Then your metabolism, glands and organs can be adversely affected and medication can have a reverse effect on your system.

Robert G. Fritchie

Another thing that happens is that some people do not trust the Creator or this Process so they try simultaneous and conflicting mental energy treatments to seek relief. If they have not learned to test truth or doubt their own Spirit, they do not learn the truth about themselves and get false energy information that is simply untrue. They may believe the input because it fortifies their belief.

This is a good place to discuss mental release techniques people use to relieve emotional issues. You are told how effective a technique is in marketing promotions. Yet there are many cases where the techniques do not work as advertised, but these cases are generally not discussed in public. *The problem is that mental techniques do not release Soul-based issues.*

A person can be born with a Soul vibration from a previous life that feeds the mind/body in this life causing many unusual behaviors and symptoms. *Soul-based problems can usually be released with the DLGHP along with the mind and body symptoms. When one lets go of fear the need to hold on to an illness dissipates.*

One Caution

Most people think they are OK and are not subject to these factors in their lives. Please do not assume that you are exempt. Release yourself from the limited beliefs identified above one at a time.

Be aware that any time you are doing self-healing, you may need to repeat a given LL Petition periodically until you are completely free of a given limitation.

Applications Of Divine Love

Personal Health

In the last few years, it seems like life is speeding up and everything is now being conducted in a frantic mode. We rush around to satisfy needs - be they ours or other people's needs.

Sometimes frantic behavior is driven by fear and spiritual blocks so severe that energy does not flow properly in the body. If Divine Love is not circulating in your system (as determined by others), stop what you are doing and address the Life Lesson topics.

Once you clear the Life Lessons you are ready to address whatever you like in a Petition for your own wellness.

How People And Events Can Affect You

One of the insidious things that can happen to you is what I call "hook effects."

When we build emotional relationships with friends, coworkers and family, an energetic bond forms between us and the person with whom we are close. That bond is like a long energetic rope with hooks on both ends. The hooks are usually attached to each person at their solar plexus. When either person reacts to an emotional situation, they pull the person on the other end of their energetic rope along with them. Their problem is now your problem!

The result is like watching a tug of war. You are on one end of *many energetic* ropes and you are being dragged around by the people on the other end of *each* rope. You have probably heard this same concept expressed in the phrase "pushing someone's buttons." One person says something that triggers a response in another person and an argument soon begins.

Some people react to *all news reports* in like manner because they are emotionally hooked to their TV, radio, telephone or friendly gossiper. If this happens to you, it is common to experience a range of overwhelming emotions that can ultimately bring you to a complete standstill! If this condition is not released, your body can overload and you can begin a downward spiral into deep anxiety, fear, depression or panic attacks.

As the years go on, you generally add more and more hooks to your body. If you are a very emotional person, the effects of your hooks amplifies and makes EVERY problem encounter seem larger to you than it is normally. Eventually your system can no longer handle the continuous bombardment of emotions and you are in trouble.

Now let's look at a hook from your end of the rope. If you are a person that wants to impart guidance to others, be careful!

If the recipient resists your counsel then the tendency is to start unconsciously transferring your emotional drivers to whomever is on the other end of the same rope! An example of this transfer occurs in parents who have an overwhelming need to try to protect their children from ugliness in the world.

It is important that we not transfer our fears and limitations to our children. We can give our children guidelines for their own protection. As our children grow we must accept that we can no longer protect them. It is time to start letting them make their own decisions.

Fortunately, you can break hooks without struggling to identify them. What you want are healthy relationships with people, but not bonds that control your every thought. In case you are wondering, releasing your hooks does not diminish the human love or other healthy bonds between people.

Apply your angel Petition with this symptom clause - *Release all my hooks attaching me to people, things and my own thoughts.*

Then sit quietly; do slow deep breathing while the hooks dissolve. This effort may take you several days when doing your Petition alone because any hooks from parents or your siblings can be attached to you very deeply from your childhood.

Also when you are working alone, you may need to repeat the Petition periodically to release all your hooks because the Petition stops when you are distracted. The release works best when you have one or more people sending you Divine Love while you are doing your Petition.

Always muscle test yourself using your spirit and Divine Love to verify that you are completely released from all hooks. Wait about one hour and test again to be sure. Be patient with yourself. If you can not completely release your hooks, join a large Group to apply more energy to the release.

Environmental Awareness

You have been given an overview of what is going on in the world. Various interested organizations are doing what they can to change existing conditions. The chaos that is happening right now will continue to happen in the foreseeable future until mankind is brought into alignment with the Creator's will.

Health conditions throughout the world may continue to worsen. Overworked facilities may not be able to keep up, even if money is available. Should you lack sufficient financial resources, your opportunity to receive timely services may be in jeopardy.

The future is up to you and to all of us. We can all utilize this spiritual Process to make real changes. That however is not the end game because *you* need to become responsible for your own health, your actions, and the preservation of the environment. Learn whatever you can about everything you eat, use and do. Then support those folks, who like you, are trying to improve human existence.

Spiritual Energy Healing

You have the right to understand that Divine Love is the most powerful healing force in the world. You have the right to use Divine Love to help yourself if you

Robert G. Fritchie

believe in the Creator. Simply follow the guidelines in this book.

Some individuals refuse to recognize the reality of Spiritual Energy Healing. Instead of dismissing this reality, educate yourself and experience the Process.

This form of healing may be all that is available to you depending upon the circumstances in which you find yourself.

This leads us to the next important realization. We must be able to function in our existing religions and societies. How we can do this is the subject of the next chapter.

Chapter 6

Spirituality Without Limits

Do not confuse religion with spirituality. No one's religion is under attack. Prayer is important, but we need to be responsible for, and aware of, many of the root causes of our illness.

The Creator wants us to be responsible for ourselves, and the earth and to participate in affecting the kinds of spiritual, mental and physical changes necessary for us to all live in peace and health.

Humanity is still not acting responsibly. If this were not so, how can you justify the accelerated rate of new illnesses confronting humanity right now? Or the fact that pollution is destroying humans, animals, plants and life across the planet.

We must apply our understanding of our Spirit and Divine Love and directed intention in a way that honors the Creator. When we do these things, we are exercising our spiritual birthright correctly. Then we are able to activate the healing process in ourselves and in the environment. *This is taking responsibility.*

One of the most limiting issues to worldwide cooperation is the attitude people have that "their way is the only way." We can no longer take this position in world society because people in other lands are part of the Creator's same spiritual community as you and me. *When we operate on a spiritual basis, we are able to transcend our religious, national and social differences and thereby achieve unity of purpose.*

What I now understand is that the Creator's Love includes every definition of love in every culture. Divine Love is the

ALL, the very fabric of our existence. We humans strive to explain as best we can what that love is and how it operates, but no one has a complete answer.

The Creator is the greatest mystery of the universe. Divine Love is the second greatest mystery. We can be defensive and argue in favor of our individual beliefs, or we can experience Divine Love in all its glory. When we do experience Divine Love, the real spiritual and physical truth is made manifest and changes can occur.

Divine Love Revealed

There are many scientific investigators trying to define this universal field of energy. It is referred to as a matrix, a super powerful energy field, super light, a free power, etc. All of these explanations are our attempts to explain to our rational minds what is real. One problem is our rational minds are not really all that rational! Following is an example of how people deny the obvious.

Robert G. Fritchie

There is a historical account of Captain Cook's arrival in Polynesia. He anchored his ship off-shore while he and some of his men rowed ashore in a smaller boat.

When he met the natives they were surprised and asked him through his interpreter how he had reached them. He pointed to his ship in the bay, but the natives could not see the ship! All they saw was a "canoe" - his rowboat, drawn up on the beach.

Having never seen a large sailing ship before, *it simply did not register in their consciousness*. For the Polynesians, the sailing vessel could not and therefore did not, even exist. The ship became real to the natives only after some of them had been on board the ship. Then suddenly, they could process this incredible sight and they could all see the ship!

Divine Love to some people is like the Polynesian natives mental construct. Folks can not see Divine Love so they choose to disregard it until they experi-

ence it. Then they may perceive it, even though they may not be able to explain their personal experience to anyone.

In the book, T*he Survivors Club* by Ben Sherwood, a similar mental construct is presented. People exiting the London Underground (subway) saw and smelled smoke, but they assumed that a fire was impossible so they walked into the fire and died.

In another study, the author reported that commercial airplane travelers were subject to a similar mental denial. Here are examples of the research conducted:

Those that *thought a plane crash* was *impossible* sat paralyzed by their disbelief when they were actually in a crash. Some would snap out of their disbelief and escape - others died.

Those people that *always* *thought survival was possible,* waited for others to tell them what to do. Some survived and some did not.

113

Robert G. Fritchie

People that _believed_ survival from a plane crash was possible planned far ahead, taking note of all the exits. They acted immediately and escaped.

Do you see the correlation to spiritual energy healing? *Many people are locked in a belief that they can not affect their own health with spiritual healing, so they don't even try to change.*

Other folks think change is possible, yet want to be shown how to proceed. Spiritual people jump at the chance to use this spiritual process to change because they believe in the Creator and the Process. Which type of person do you think you are?

Now let's explore an even broader view. There has been talk for years about extraterrestrial beings contacting humans and walking among us. Many people scoff at this, thinking it impossible. Yet many scientists consider that there is life on other planets and in other galaxies.

For any of us to think that we are a superior intelligence and that only earthlings have the intelligence to go to another planet is very limited thinking.

Suppose it is the other way around and that alien visitors have the more advanced civilization and technology.

How do you think our perceptions about the Divine would be affected if aliens drop out of the sky for a visit as in the 2009 television show "V"? Would such an alien intelligence have the same perceptions about the Divine as do we, or would they have a different view?

The possibilities are exciting for some humans, but very frightening to anyone being "yanked" out of their current reality. We might even act like the Polynesian natives and deny, or not even see, a spaceship hovering overhead!

Since the Creator exists in all galaxies, Divine Love is not unique to earth. It is just as present in another star system as it is here on Earth. This also means that beings from other planets are just as much our spiritual brothers and sisters as those people that we interact with on earth. We are all part of the same creation and part of the same Creator.

While it will be interesting to see what the future holds, we cannot sit idly by while our world decays. We need to be aware of how to make changes in ourselves and our environment should we choose to do so.

Chapter 7

Mechanisms For Change

What Happens If

Various authors have been making a case for an energetic shift coming to the earth that will change the vibration of our existence. Let's assume that these events are true and see what it really means to you and me. Some authors claim that such a shift even ushers in a new age of existence, but for whom?

If a sudden increase in energy occurs on earth what will be the effect on the human body? If we are already adversely impacted by chemicals, pollution, radiation and thought, will such a change

Robert G. Fritchie

enhance or hurt our existence?

My opinion is that if you have cleared the nine Life Lessons given in Chapter 5 so that you can process Divine Love throughout your entire body, then you have nothing to worry about. You will experience the future in a balanced and loving way.

If you live in fear, foster disbelief and hang on to self-defeating beliefs, your system may not be able to process Divine Love and you may experience difficulty.

Be Vigilant About Your Energy Condition

When your body stays filled with Divine Love, your body can heal as discussed previously. However, if you *disconnect* yourself from Divine Love then healing stops.

Any time that you experience a negative event, you can cut yourself off from taking in Divine Love. This can happen if you are frightened by something, made angry, or are otherwise upset. In fact, just sitting around thinking about your negative thoughts can cause you to disconnect from Divine Love!

Reconnecting To Divine Love

Reconnecting yourself to Divine Love is surprisingly easy. Simply take in a deep breath, hold your breath and recite the first part of the standard Petition as follows:

With my Spirit and the angels help, I accept Divine Love and focus Divine Love into my thymus.

Then let your breath out slowly. Repeat this simple mini-Petition any time that you start to feel unloving or have sudden emotions.

How A Petition Works

If you do take time to do the necessary Petitions does that mean you will regain perfect health? It depends. Divine Love in conjunction with a Petition of the type we teach is designed to help you implement your spiritual healing. Your Petition operates within you and runs to completion, provided that you continue to take in Divine Love to energize the Petition.

Your Petition, in conjunction with your Spirit, identifies the problem to be corrected. It is Divine Love that does the healing for you.

To the extent that your Petition matches the Creator's will for your life, your Petition will be answered and you will usually see change. If the Creator has other plans for you, then you and your Group should respect the Creator's will. However, this does NOT mean that you stop seeking the cause of a health problem. Try other Petitions to clear up a symptom as explained in Chapter 5.

It is rare that the Creator stops us from attaining our goals with Divine Love provided that we are not trying to manipulate people or a situation to satisfy our desires. Illness is a teaching not a punishment. Healing is also a teaching.

Do not forget the "G" in the DLGHP. If you can not free yourself by acting alone while using a DLGHP based angel Petition, then seek a Group and work with that Group.

The Power Of Focused Divine Love

Pain Control

Once you realize that the DLGHP is truly a *spiritual* process and not a mental exercise, it is possible for you to do things that you would not have thought possible. For example, if you suddenly experience a pain - use your spirit and Divine Love to focus directly on the pain source until the pain breaks. You can do the same thing for sudden stress.

Robert G. Fritchie

Accurate Muscle Testing

For many years, we have taught people how to do muscle testing. You can learn how to test in *Surviving Chaos*.

In all the years of teaching, only a few people did not get truthful results using muscle testing. One woman's answers would always test false to any question known to be true. She asked me a legitimate question: "How can I trust my results?" I knew that her mind was interfering with her muscle test.

I also knew that *an individual's Spirit always gives correct answers AND corrects any measurement problem with Divine Love*, so I told her to preface any muscle test with a simple *mini-Petition*:

With my Spirit and Divine Love I conduct this test. Is (test topic) true?

The mini-Petition always gave her correct answers and it will help you to avoid interference from your mind. As her measurement problem cleared, she was able to get accurate answers without using the mini-Petition.

To be sure that you are getting truthful answers, run a calibration test. Since we all know that drinking six shots of whiskey in a row is bad for us, we can form a test question like this:

Is taking six shots of whiskey in fifteen minutes good for me?

If the answer is *yes*, then you know that your system is out of balance and that you need to use the *mini-Petition* to get accurate answers.

Using the following mini-Petition should give you a "no" answer:

With my Spirit and Divine Love I conduct this test. Is taking six shots of whiskey in fifteen minutes good for me?

Robert G. Fritchie

Muscle Test Everything

By using your spirit with Divine Love to muscle test, you can ask yourself if a certain product is safe for you to consume. You can also determine the exact dosage of vitamins, minerals or over the counter health products that you plan to use. The same testing applies to the foods you eat and other products you use on, or in your body.

Get The Spiritual Truth

Again: If you have a long-term problem, be it spiritual, mental or physical, you can use a simple Petition to attempt a self-healing correction. If that does not yield results, run a muscle test to learn what needs to be done and in what order you should proceed. Then go to a Group to get the energy boost needed to correct your problem.

The greatest problem people seem to have is NOT some Process mechanism needed for health recovery. Rather, it is their ability to set aside what they think is their rational mental thought process and start to trust their own spirit.

Very few teachers have offered the general public a spiritual healing process that actually works. Teachers who stay focused on mind and body concepts are missing the opportunity to teach this all encompassing healing system.

Your spirit is given to you by the Creator and is your personal link to the Creator. It is part of you, not apart from you.

Your spirit is not an alien spirit attached to torment you. Your spirit is present to help you and to guide you.

Be assured that your own spirit will not lie to you, whereas your mind may mislead you based upon the repository of thoughts stored in the mind.

The mind reinforces your situation, be it good or bad. Thus, breaking unwanted patterns in your life can be difficult if you use mental techniques. This is because mind resists change even though that change may be good for you. That is why we all need to take a leap of faith and trust our own spirit.

Some individuals trying to connect with their spirit for guidance report that their mind chatters away in the background.

Spirit tells you what you need to do.

Mind tells you what you want to hear.

The way to get mind out of the way is to *use Divine Love in a conversation with your spirit because <u>Divine Love allows only the truth to come through.</u>* Any foreign input or mind interference is bypassed. This is another important spiritual teaching for you to learn.

If you are stuck in a mental quandary and want to get free from your problem, you need to learn how to start a dialog with your own spirit. That is done by a declarative intention on your part to set the proper stage for the conversation. I use:

With my spirit I focus Divine Love into my thymus. I ask...

Then I start to ask for guidance. I always get an answer unless the answer had been previously given to me. The key is not to analyze the guidance because it may be altogether different than what you are asking.

For example, let's say that you are very frightened. You might be tempted to use a Petition that addresses "fright" as the symptom to use in a Petition. However, when you ask for guidance, your spirit, being all wise, might tell you to release "unlovingness toward yourself" followed by "forgiving" someone.

If you try to mentally analyze that guidance you might say to yourself: "This cannot be. I love myself. I have forgiven everyone in my life." Then you might reject the advice of your spirit and charge off in a different direction that does not provide a solution.

In the example given spirit is saying:

1. Do two things.

2. Do them in the order given.

The unstated part of the guidance is—don't embellish what is given or append other symptoms to your Petition now.

Go slowly and follow your internal spiritual guidance.

About Personal Power

When people surrender themselves to be controlled by others, it is referred to as giving up their personal power. This is a familiar term for many women who see themselves as the only cohesive factor in their families.

This is fine provided that one does not

lose one's own identity by being a caregiver to everyone else while not taking care of oneself.

If you do not place value on yourself, it often results in emotional disorders because you are suppressing your true self in an effort to make others happy.

Fortunately people can recover their own identities, personal power, and sense of self-worth, but it takes a particular effort to do so. That effort is to learn to trust and work with your spirit to recover your health.

Your future is up to you. Apply the principles of spirit and Divine Love and then watch as your world changes for the better.

Robert G. Fritchie

Chapter 8

Putting it All Together

Virtual Healing Group

In October 2009, we started a series of public webinars that people could attend as anonymous Volunteers. This was and is a Group effort to provide worldwide healing based upon the principles described in *Surviving Chaos: Healing With Divine Love*.

A webinar is a seminar style Internet meeting in which Volunteers can see, hear and participate in spiritual healing programs for themselves, humanity and the environment. We call our webinars Conference Calls.

Participants have joined us from Japan, Europe, Canada, Mexico, Australia, the United States and South America. All of the programs are well-attended and our participants enjoy the Calls.

Participants know that it is with groups of spiritual people working together with Divine Love and a Petition that changes can be facilitated throughout the world.

The programs are:

Mass Consciousness and Environmental Problems Conference Calls

Mass consciousness is the collection of thought energy from people. One might think that the mass consciousness is so large that changing anything in it would be impossible. Such is not the case because Divine Love can change anything. When we operate as a Group on this Call we can help to make a difference!

This is a weekly one-hour Call. The objective is to energetically correct problems in the mass consciousness and environmental problems that threaten the well-being of human beings. We focus on two aspects:

Increasing awareness about selected problems and then *conducting spiritual energy healings* on those problems for the highest good of all people.

As we undertook more difficult topics, we saw that some weeks we did not have sufficient Group energy to complete a healing in a reasonable time. On just one problem alone, we spent four, one-hour Calls serving a single country!

To decrease the time factor and to have the group spiritual energy be more effective, we asked for help from all of the Creator's angels. Most of our Volunteers felt a major shift in energy take place with angelic support. We observed that we could then serve a much larger geographical *area* of the world in *five to ten minutes rather than hours.*

The angels energetic boost enabled us to combine adjacent countries that enabled us to then segment the world into ten geographical areas. We did this so that Volunteers could experience the energy effects applied to different areas of the world. Now in *one hour*, we can generally go through ten geographical areas in two passes:

The first pass is to improve *awareness*. The second pass is to *spiritually heal a problem* energetically with Divine Love.

Who benefits from this activity? The answer is every human being that is willing to accept Divine Love into their lives!

Individual Healing Conference Calls

This is a separate Group healing session composed of Volunteers. Groups consist of human Volunteers and the Creator's angels. We utilize Divine Love and a Petition to help individual recipients that are seeking help.

Robert G. Fritchie

Generally we help individuals that have not been able to attain relief by other means.

Since our recipients apply for help from many countries, we require that each recipient become familiar with the Process (DLGHP) and submit a statement concerning their symptoms before we accept them on the Call. We do this because many people do not have any prior experience with spiritual healing. We want them to understand the fundamentals so that they can more effectively participate.

Some of our more difficult cases required that prerequisite problems concerning the Chapter 5 Life Lessons be addressed before a recipient's initial Petition was granted by the Creator. Once people understood the principles and then cleared themselves of the issues identified in the nine Spiritual Life Lessons, they began to experience change. In fact many of their old symptoms disappeared as they proceeded through the

134

Life Lessons!

Training Conference Calls

This is a course that contains both basic and advanced healing techniques to better prepare a student to do Group and individual healing work. Students learn how to experience and measure energy and develop their intuition and skills.

Particular emphasis is given to understanding the differences in energy techniques using spirit, soul, mind and body in healing efforts. It is a highly experiential course.

Our Wish For You

People are being confronted by *changes* in weather, services, jobs and health. If you do not have a way to help yourself, then consider the Spiritual system being talked about in this book. The Divine Love Group Healing Process is given to you with love and without cost. It works and it is there for your use. Download a

Robert G. Fritchie

free copy from our web site.

We are working together as an international community to help apply the principles of Divine Love in ways to help humanity.

We hope that you join us as a Volunteer
and help make a difference.

Appendix

Why Industrial Pollution Corrections Are Slow

I was a consulting engineering manager in one of the top 40 consulting engineering firms in the mid 70's. Many of my clients were industrial companies struggling to do the right thing. Their primary business was to manufacture goods.

As emphasis on environmental control became popular, many companies were caught in a difficult situation. Pollution control solutions for air and water quality improvements could cost millions of dollars per plant. Capital investment in these solutions hurt companies financially, but corrections had to be made to avoid plant closures and noncompliance

137

financial fines.

Had environmental corrections been applied worldwide, price balance in world markets might have been maintained. However, with increasing costs and decreasing prices, certain U.S. companies doing business internationally could not compete profitably.

The steel industry is a case in point. To raise revenues, several steel manufactures sold their manufacturing technology to Asian countries. U.S. companies soon learned that Asian manufacturers could sell Asian steel in the U.S. at very low prices. Unable to compete, many of our domestic steel plants failed, were sold or absorbed by other companies.

The paper industry is another example. As electronic media gained acceptance, demand for newsprint declined and paper company profits shrank. As environmental regulations increased, the paper companies spent millions of dollars to become pollution compliant. Eventually the price vs. cost strain put many paper companies out of business.

Power plant companies also suffered. They were required to provide air and water pollution systems on both new and existing plants. There was less financial impact among power plants because they could pass on some costs to their customer base.

Earlier we talked about toxins getting into our foods. The food industry suffers similar cost challenges as they strive to meet consumer safety regulations. As the cost of their manufactured goods rises, and prices decline, small food companies have difficulty being profitable.

The answer for many companies, regardless of industry, has been to transfer their capital dollars to foreign countries. Then the companies can manufacture in countries with less environmental constraints and lower manufacturing costs.

Robert G. Fritchie

As a result of this manufacturing change the United States has become a consumer country that imports many goods and services while manufacturing less. In the expanding foreign countries, pollution is increasing and the residents are being adversely affected where pollution solutions have not been applied.

About The Author

Bob Fritchie enjoyed a forty-year career as both a professional chemical engineer and business manager.

In 1979 Bob formed a lifelong friendship with Marcel Vogel, a world renowned IBM scientist. Marcel, Bob and a team of dedicated professionals put together a research laboratory in San Jose, California. Once in place, the lab team began a scientific study of subtle energy healing principles. Bob served on the Board of Directors and as business manager for the lab.

Marcel, Bob and others affiliated with the lab taught the emerging energy principles through workshops to help people heal their lives and health problems. The key teachings were based upon recognizing that the Creator's love is real and can be experienced in our lives to heal us.

Bob formed World Service Institute as a nonprofit, nondenominational teaching company to help the general public understand and apply Divine Love in the resolution of problems.

Contacting Us

Bob can be reached by email at:
healinghelp@worldserviceinstitute.org

Visit the World Service Institute website at: http://www.worldserviceinstitute.org

Publications

To date there are three books available to the public:

Surviving Chaos: Healing With Divine Love
Minimize Your Surgical and Rehabilitation Pain
Apply Your Birthright - A Spiritual

Solution to Your Health and Environmental Problems

These books can be purchased on-line through Amazon and at many other on-line booksellers throughout the world.

World Service Institute does not sell directly to the public. We operate exclusively through bookstores and distributors. Ask your local bookstore to order copies through the 2009 and 2010 edition of Books In Print.

CPSIA information can be obtained at www.ICGtesting.com
Printed in the USA
LVOW12s0830040813

346134LV00001B/41/P